Learning About Mission

Mission Matters!

John D. Brand

Christian Focus

To my parents
who, in the providence of God,
gave me the inestimable privilege
of beginning life on the mission field

ISBN 1 85792 4029

© John Brand
First published in 1999
by
Christian Focus Publications
Geanies House, Fearn,
Ross-shire, IV20 1TW, Great Britain

Cover design by Owen Daily

Contents

INTRODUCTION

The title of this little book is deliberately ambiguous. It not only describes the contents but makes a statement. Mission matters! World mission is very much the poor relation of church life in our country in these days, and many churches and Christian leaders fail, not only to grasp the importance of mission and its centrality to the Word of God, but also miss out on the great joy and blessing that comes from involvement in fulfilling the Great Commission of Christ – to 'go and make disciples of all nations'.

This book is in no way meant to be an exhaustive study on the subject of world mission, far less the last word on the subject. The contents first saw the light of day as the basis of midweek Bible studies in the church where I was pastor, and then, in a revised form, as a package I presented in a number of churches. The idea behind them was simply to bring before God's people a reminder of the importance and challenge of world mission, and stimulate some reaction.

Over the years, as I have read, studied and worked in the whole area of mission, I have gleaned quotes, comments and facts – not all of which I have been able to trace to their source. If I have unwittingly quoted or borrowed without due acknowledgement, then the fault is mine, though unintentional.

John D Brand

1

GOING BY THE BOOK

The Biblical Basis of Mission

A. The motives for mission

If you were to ask serving missionaries why they had chosen that particular sphere of service, I suspect that you would get a wide variety of responses. People are motivated to mission, as to other areas of Christian life, by a whole range of motives, some purer and higher than others. I have personally met a missionary serving overseas who admitted that he was doing so because it would look good on his CV and enhance his job prospects when he would return home. Others, perhaps, get involved because of the opportunity it provides to travel to interesting parts of the world and experience different cultures. I have no doubt that some, albeit mistakenly, see it as a soft option to the 'real world' back at home. None of these motives are worthy of the cause of the gospel and those offering themselves for service on the basis of these motives should have been sifted out early on in their application procedures.

There are two worthy and biblical motives, however, that we should examine and which should be uppermost in the hearts and minds of anyone considering the possibility of missionary service.

A passion for people

No Christian will ever be truly effective as a missionary unless he has a genuine love and concern for those he seeks to serve. You cannot read the letters written by the apostle Paul to the young churches which had been founded during his missionary travels without feeling something of his fervent love for the men and women to whom he went with the gospel.

Even stronger is the passion in the heart of the Saviour as he moved among men and women in all their need. Yet, what moved the Lord more than the sickness, poverty and oppression of the people of his day was their spiritual need – 'they were harassed and helpless, like sheep without a shepherd' (Matt. 9:36). The spiritual lostness of men and women may not be as visible and prominent as their physical hunger and disease yet it is of far greater consequence and we dare not ignore it.

One of the most destructive influences on the missionary emphasis of the church in recent years has been the inroads made by liberal theology and pluralistic philosophies which have questioned the need for personal salvation, denied the doctrine of eternal punishment and undermined the uniqueness of Jesus Christ, making him one of numerous, equally legitimate and effective mediators of salvation. It is interesting to note that, as these views have taken hold in many circles, the churches espousing them have produced less and less missionaries. In fact 90% of 'career missionaries' on the field today are from conservative evangelical denominations or independent evangelical missionary agencies.

As John Stott says, 'It is an observable fact of history, both past and contemporary, that the degree of the church's commitment to world evangelisation is commensurate with the degree of its conviction about the authority of the Bible. Whenever Christians lose their confidence in the Bible they also lose their zeal for evangelism. Conversely, whenever they are convinced about the Bible, then they are determined about evangelism.'[1]

Traditional teaching about Christ being the only way to God, the exclusiveness of the gospel and the reality of the horrors of hell and eternal damnation may not be attractive and palatable but they are biblical and we have no right to water them down or ignore them.

Yet, some of those who would call themselves evangelicals are lining up to soft pedal these clear Scriptural teachings. Here are just two examples:

'It would seem consistent...with God's gracious activity, that those who have not heard of Christ in the centuries since Calvary could also wake up on the other side of death to find themselves accepted with God.'

'It may be possible for some to respond to the knowledge of God that they have and to cross over the bridge of Christ without realising that this vital bridge is even there.'

The truth is, of course, that if a single man, woman or young person should be saved without a personal experience of the crucified Saviour, then the cross is an appalling and unnecessary waste. Would God have given up the Son of his love as a substitutionary sacrifice for sinners if there was some other way for them to be saved? Of course not. Was Jesus Christ, the Son of God, mistaken, or, even worse, lying when he asserted, 'no one comes to the Father but by me'? Of course not. Jesus is the way, the only way to God, and without consciously coming by way of the cross, there is no salvation.

As I was finishing this manuscript, I came across a book by Hywel Jones who argues more cogently and theologically than I ever could for the traditional, biblical position on the exclusiveness of the gospel and the necessity of hearing the good news in order to be saved. Let me give you some of his final words:

> As he was about to leave this earth and return to heaven, the Lord commanded his apostles, and through them his church, to 'go and make disciples of all nations, baptising them in the name of the Father and of the Son and of the Holy Spirit'. Did he send them on an unnecessary task, a fool's errand? or is their going out into all the world with the gospel as essential in its own way, as was his coming down into it?...
>
> Will more people go to the mission field? What kind of people will go? Will they be like Judson, Carey, Paton, Moffatt, Martyn, Studd,

Hudson Taylor?... Evangelical optimists [by which Jones means those who leave open the possibility that some will be saved without hearing of and believing in Christ] say their position is not detrimental to the spread of the gospel; but that claim has a hollow ring. The proof is otherwise.

The history of world mission bears forceful witness here. The era of missionary concern and expansion rose out of the Great Awakening associated with Whitefield and the Wesleys at the end of the eighteenth century. When that blessing shook down the churches, Christians were shaken up and 'the world became their parish'. By contrast, the churches in the western world are in decline not only numerically and financially but morally, doctrinally and spiritually. Is this a time to argue for the salvation of the unevangelised? Is it not rather a time to assert the necessity of taking the gospel where 'Christ is not named?'[2]

There is also a move within evangelicalism to deny the truth of eternal punishment. Some would have us preach 'punishment in eternity', which conveniently sidesteps the moral dilemma of why a supposedly loving God should consign to and keep a large proportion of mankind in endless, conscious torment. Yet the doctrine of eternal damnation, however horrific and unpleasant, has been a stimulus behind the missionary movement from the days of

Paul to William Carey and beyond. Cotton Mather, an American contemporary of George Whitefield, used to preach 'the terrors' before preaching 'the comforts', warning people of the wrath to come before explaining the way of escape provided in Christ.

What Hudson Taylor wrote about China in 1894 can still be said of many places in the world more than one hundred years later: 'There is a great Niagara of souls passing into the dark in China. Every day, every week, every month they are passing away! A million a month in China are dying without God.'

The truth is that if I do not really believe in my heart of hearts that if a man or woman dies without a personal experience of and having been saved by the Lord Jesus Christ, the worst that awaits them beyond this life – if indeed there is anything – is some form of annihilation, then I am not going to risk life and limb or put myself to considerable inconvenience or sacrifice material comforts and a promising career to go and tell them what they do not really need to hear. Let them eat, drink and be merry, if there is no hell to face.

If, as a lecturer in a leading UK Bible College recently assured his students, Muslims who remain faithful to their beliefs throughout their lives are eternally safe, as are Jews and all devout religious people, then we should call home every missionary serving overseas and stop wasting our time and money.

If, on the other hand, I am utterly convinced that

what really awaits the lost are the indescribable horrors of hell – a conscious yet Christless eternity, then I will do all in my power, either to warn them myself or support and enable someone else to do so.

Supposing I know my neighbours to be asleep in their beds when I notice that their house is burning fiercely in the middle of the night. Do I worry myself as to whether they will take kindly to be woken by my hammering on the door and disturbing their sleep? Do I comfort myself with the thought that the fire or its accompanying smoke will cause their deaths quite quickly, so they won't suffer too much? No, I will do everything in my power to arouse them to their fate and call to their assistance anyone who has the power to help. Yet millions live and die, passing into the unquenchable fires of hell without any note of warning being sounded by those who are aware of their plight but do not appear to care.

We have, to a large extent, lost our passion for mission because we have lost our passion for men and women, not really believing that living and dying without Christ they pass into a lost eternity

A passion for God

The motive we have just considered is a worthy one and certainly a biblical one, but it is not the highest one. There is something else that should move us out even when we lack the concern we ought to feel for those who are outside of Christ. It is a passion for God. Indeed, my contention is that we have lost our passion for the spiritual well-being of men and women because we have lost our passion for the honour and glory of God.

John Stott, commenting on the New Testament accounts of the missionary activities of the early Christians, says, 'They knew that God had superexalted Jesus, enthroning him at his right hand and bestowing upon him the highest rank, in order that every tongue should confess his Lordship. They longed that Jesus should receive the honour due to his name.'[3]

Here surely is what mission is all about. It is, as the psalmist puts it, 'declaring the glory of God to the nations of the world' (Ps. 96:3). Peter Beyerhaus puts it this way:

'We are called and sent to glorify the reign of God and to manifest his saving work before the whole world... Today it is extremely important to emphasize the priority of this doxological aim before all other aims of mission. Our one-sided concern with man and his society threatens to pervert mission and make it a secular or even a quasi-atheistic undertaking. We are living in an age of apostasy where man arrogantly makes himself the measuring rod of all things. Therefore, it is a part of our missionary task courageously to confess before all enemies of the cross that the earth belongs to God and to his anointed... Our task in mission is to uphold the banner of the risen Lord before the whole world, because it is his own.'[4]

A couple of years ago, having preached in a church in Edinburgh, I was standing at the door shaking hands with the congregation as they left, when a very small boy, aged about four, stood almost on my toes with his eyes boring into my knee-caps – I am about six feet three inches tall. He gradually lifted his eyes to my head and, either with his lips or expression exclaimed, 'Wow, he's big!' I feel we need to regain something of that childlike wonder and awe about our great and glorious God. Having reminded ourselves just how 'big' he is, we will then be more enthusiastic about telling others. The small, frustrated, feeble God that so many Christians seem to believe in today hardly inspires evangelistic enthusiasm and missionary mobilisation.

In his book, *A Vision for Missions*, Tom Wells recalls the passion of David Brainerd, the missionary to the North American Indians.

'Brainerd prays for his friends and his enemies. But this act of prayer rises out of a higher vision. God must be known, and not simply by name. God's name was well-known, even in the wilds of New Jersey. God must be known as GOD! To Brainerd that was the great thing. Even Christ's kingdom serves that end. Let God be known! To know God is the great essential. And to make him known was Brainerd's task.'[5]

We need to regain our passion and enthusiasm for this great, this uniquely glorious God, and we need to become jealous for his glory, even as God is jealous for his own glory. After all, while men and women, created in the image of God to glorify and enjoy him for ever, give this devotion to anyone or anything else, God is not honoured as he deserves.

Neither will God be fully and worthily honoured and glorified until men and women from every nation, tribe, people and language join in the everlasting song of praise to the Lamb of God. The church's mandate, the Great Commission, is to 'declare his glory among the nations (people groups)' (Ps. 96:3) of the world so that the untold diversity of the peoples of the world, united in praise to God, echo the depth and greatness of God's glory. God is glorified and honoured when he is worshipped by many of the 12,000 peoples of the world, as he is today, but not as much as he will be when all those groups, including the 3,000 among whom there is at present little if any Christian witness, are represented around the throne.

The correct translation of Revelation 21:3 is not 'they will be his people' but 'they will be his *peoples*, and God himself will be with them and be their God.' We sometimes sing of heaven – and it's perfectly true – 'O that will be glory for me.'

B. The mandate for mission

It is, or at least it ought to be, the unashamed testimony of God's people that we engage in mission because God has told us to. The Great Commission, as we call it, at the end of Jesus' earthly ministry, laid on God's people for all time the duty of taking the good news of the gospel to all the peoples of the world. However, the theme of world mission does not begin with the New Testament. It begins at the very opening of the Scriptures and is woven into the whole of God's Word. The Bible – the whole Bible – is the story of world mission, the unfolding revelation of God's heart for all his world through the pages of Scripture. We cannot begin, in a book of this size or nature, to give an exhaustive list of biblical references on the subject of world mission, but we can highlight a few of them to help us see the all-pervasive nature of this theme in the pages of Scripture. We will inescapably discover that 'All the world is in all the Word'.

Abraham
Genesis 12:1-3: After generations of silence following the fall and its consequences, God again broke into human history. He gave to Abraham a promise of new dealings with mankind and began to reveal his plans for blessing the nations of the world. Four more times God repeated this revelation – twice to Abraham (Gen. 15:1-5; 22:18), once to Isaac (Gen. 26:4), and once to Jacob (Gen. 28:14). 'It was as if he wanted to underline his message: "I have a heart for the nations and I'm not going to rest until men from every people know my friendship".'[6]

Moses

Exodus 19:5-6: Then followed the period of slavery in Egypt, and the next stage of God's unfolding purposes came through Moses, when God promised that, through the people of Israel – a priestly people – the whole earth would be blessed.

The prophets

The prophetic messages are strewn with promises from God that there was to be a world-wide gathering in of the nations into the heavenly kingdom with an eternal King. The great King David was a foreshadowing of God's ultimate purposes. Among many world view references in the prophetic writings are the following: Isaiah 9:1-2; Joel 2:32 and Malachi 1:10-11.

The psalms

Many of the psalms take up this great world-wide vision as well, e.g.: 2:8; 22:27; 67:2; 72:9; 96:3; 102:15.

Jesus' ministry

Jesus, in his own ministry, demonstrated that the gospel was for a far wider audience than merely the Jews. Note, for example, his visits to Gadara and the Samaritans.

But, most importantly of all, he gives his 'Great Commission', repeated no less than five times in the first five books of the New Testament (Matthew 28:19-20; Mark 16:15; Luke 24:46-49; John 20:21; Acts 1:8).

Acts

Edmund Clowney writes, 'It seems almost incredible that with the Book of Acts in the Scriptures the church could ever have lost sight of its mission.'[7] The whole record of Acts is a gradual fulfilment of Jesus' prophetic command in Acts 1:8:

Acts 1–7 relates the growth of the church in Jerusalem.

Acts 8–12 sees the church expand into Judea and Samaria.

Acts 13–28 traces the rapid advance of the gospel, mainly through the ministry of Paul, into the nations of the world.

It is also interesting to note that the only stories repeated in detail within the book are Peter's vision of the 'unclean' being acceptable to God (given twice) and Paul's call to the Gentiles (given three times). The climax of the book comes when Paul finally reaches Rome and repeats his statement that the Gentiles rather than the Jews will listen.

The epistles

The epistles have been described as 'basically missionary letters written from a missionary (or missionaries) to young Christians who were becoming established in their faith'.[8] They certainly lay bare for us the heart of the great missionary traveller, Paul.

Independently and collectively they take up the theme of God's desire for 'all men to be saved and to come to a knowledge of the truth' (1 Tim. 2:4 cp. Eph. 3:8; Col. 1:6; 2 Pet. 3:9).

Revelation

Revelation 5:9-10; 7:9-10, for example. Here all God's purposes come to fulfilment and we have a glimpse of the time when it will all be completed. There gathered around the throne of heaven will be men and women from 'every nation, tribe, people and tongue'.

So the Scriptures not only contain the message for world mission, they also contain our mandate. As you read the Scriptures as a whole you become increasingly aware of a God whose heart encompasses the whole human race and whose longing is that all men and women, regardless of national, tribal, ethnic or linguistic distinction, should hear of his Son, the Lord Jesus Christ. It was as William Carey, often called the father of modern missions, read the Bible that 'he became convinced that foreign missions were the central responsibility of the church'.[9]

Yet it would appear that many Christians read and study their Bibles with such narrow perspectives, only looking for what God has to say to them in their individual circumstances; so they fail to grasp the breadth of the vision and the beat of the heart of the author of Scripture. It is possible today to go right through theological institutions here in the West and apparently study the Scriptures in depth and fail to see it from a world perspective. I could personally introduce you to ministers who have completed their theological training without having any exposure to the teaching and challenge of world mission. Having noted the constantly recurring theme of mission in the Scriptures, it is quite an achievement to spend three or four years studying God's Word without any world-wide relevance. No wonder many pastors and preachers are not bringing to the attention of their listeners the challenge of God's Word to 'declare his glory among the nations'. As Martin Goldsmith puts it, 'Why do many ministers fail to teach world missions in their regular Bible exposition? Why do students fail to pass on this vision to new Christians? Why do many Christians of all ages consider overseas mission to be an optional extra? The fundamental reason is that they do not see it as a basic teaching of the whole of Scripture. It is a failure to grasp the biblical basis of mission that stops it being taught in the normal everyday programme of Bible teaching.'[10]

David Howard has written, 'The missionary enterprise of the church is not a pyramid built upside down with its point on one isolated text in the New Testament, out of which we have built a huge structure known as "missions". Rather, the missionary enterprise of the church is a great pyramid built right side up with its base running from Genesis 1 to Revelation 22. All of Scripture forms the foundation for the outreach of the gospel to the whole world.'[11]

God's Word is, in many ways, a mission manual, God's mission manual, revealing how he set about and is accomplishing the evangelising of the nations of the world. Mission is the thread that holds together all the individual truths of Scripture.

C. The means of mission
Throughout the Bible, God's continuing and unchanging purpose is clear: 'For the earth will be filled with the knowledge of the glory of the LORD as the waters cover the sea' (Hab. 2:14).

But we can discern a development in God's strategy. In the Old Testament, working through Israel, God's mission strategy was mainly in people being *brought in* to the body of the redeemed (Exod. 12:38; Lev. 17:8). There were, of course, some notable exceptions, like the reluctant Jonah who was called to go as a missionary to call the Ninevites to repentance.

In the New Testament, the responsibility was transferred to the new tenants of God's vineyard – the church – and here the emphasis is on his people being *sent out*. The church is God's appointed agency for carrying out this eternal purpose. There are all sorts of 'optional extras' that churches may or may not take on board, but there are some things that are fundamental to the very nature of the church. We couldn't imagine a healthy church that didn't meet on the Lord's Day for worship and teaching, or that didn't meet at some other time for fellowship, study and prayer etc. Neither should we contemplate a church without a world view and a mission strategy. It is part and parcel of what a church is.

The church is central in God's missionary

purpose and must not pass that responsibility to others. A correct biblical view of the church helps us to have a correct, biblical view of mission. Missionary work is to be church-centred if it is to be effective and God-honouring. Missionaries do not, or at least should not, venture out as 'lone rangers' or 'free agents', but as those recognised and commissioned by their own churches. The local church knows the members to release for overseas service and those to keep at home. It can work with missionary societies who have expertise, resources and structures etc. but it must not delegate the responsibility of world mission to them. Missionary agencies have an obligation not to usurp the authority of the local church and its spiritual leadership over their serving missionaries. Missionaries should not be accepted, or even considered, without the full knowledge, involvement and support of the church of which they are members. It saddens me when I hear, as I did recently, of a minister being advised by a mission agency that one of his members had been accepted for overseas service on the day he had received a letter asking for a personal reference, with the assurance that his views and that of the church would be taken into consideration. God's intent is that 'through the church, the manifold wisdom of God should be made known to the rulers and authorities in the heavenly realms' (Eph. 3:10).

D. The mistakes about mission

Given the clear, consistent teaching of God's Word about world mission, it seems astonishing that there is so little concern for it among the average, evangelical churchgoer in the West today. In my personal experience, both as a pastor and a missionary speaker, missionary meetings are the worst attended in the church's diary, worse even than the regular prayer meeting. Many ministers will view the visit of a missionary speaker as the opportunity for a 'night off', conveying to his congregation the impression that it is of little importance. Why is this so? As I shared the initial notes of this book with a friend, his reply to this question was, 'because too many mission presentations are so boring!' I can't argue with that. As a pastor I have sat through all too many dull and uninteresting missionary meetings and my philosophy is that 'a bad missionary meeting is worse than no missionary meeting at all'. But there are, undoubtedly more fundamental causes of this lamentable lack of concern for that which is of such great concern to God?

We have already looked at one, possibly the most fundamental of all, the lack of conviction about certain foundational biblical truths. There are at least four others that we should take note of.

1. Misconception as to the character of the Christian life
One of the most telling illustrations used in the Bible to depict the Christian life is that of warfare. Yet we have so often failed to impress on new converts that

the new life on which they have embarked is not supposed to be a life of luxury and ease but one of continued struggle and conflict. The maintenance of the faith and the advancement of the kingdom of God demands a continual fight, as texts such as Colossians 1:29: 'To this end I labour, struggling with all his energy'; Colossians 4:12: Epaphras 'is always wrestling in prayer for you'; and Hebrews 4:11: 'Let us, therefore, make every effort to enter that rest', bear witness. We need to get our Christians and our churches on a war footing; to see every new Christian as an enlisted soldier.

'In wartime the newspapers carry headlines about how the troops are doing. In wartime families talk about the sons and daughters on the front lines and write to them and pray for them with heart-wrenching concern for their safety. In wartime we are on the alert. We are armed. We are vigilant. In wartime we spend money differently – there is austerity, not for its own sake, but because there are more strategic ways to spend money than on new tires at home. The war effort touches everybody. We all cut back. The luxury liner becomes a troop carrier.

'Very few people think that we are in a war that is greater than World War II, or any imaginable nuclear war. Few reckon that Satan is a much worse enemy than any earthly foe, or realise that the conflict is not restricted to any one global theatre, but is in every town and city in the world. Who considers that the casualties of this war do not merely lose an arm or an eye or an earthly life, but lose everything, even their own soul and enter a hell of everlasting torment?'[12]

If we truly shared God's heart for the lost of this world and were utterly convinced of their eternal fate then we would stop pampering ourselves with luxuries and spending ever increasing amounts of time and money on ourselves. Our churches would no longer be comfortable hotels and would become barracks and military outposts from which war was waged against the enemy.

Yet, here in the UK, Christians gather together, it would seem in ever larger numbers, for celebration gatherings, worship meetings and huge conferences and yet show little appetite and enthusiasm for events where they will be exposed to and challenged by the spiritual plight of millions who live in our world.

2. Misunderstanding as to the condition of the world
As I travel around and speak about world mission today I am frequently alarmed when I realise how little the average Christian and churchgoer knows about the world, in spiritual terms at least. There is a general feeling that the age of mission is now finished and that almost all have had a chance to hear the gospel. The truth is very different.

The sobering truth is that at the end of the twentieth century, nearly one in four of the present population of this world has yet to hear the good news of the gospel. That represents around 1.5 billion people who live and die in complete ignorance of the message of salvation that so many of us have known for generations. Almost a quarter of all the 12,000 people groups or tribes in the world are still without a Christian witness, many of them held fast in the great spiritual blocs of Islam, Hinduism and the Eastern religions.

Islam accounts for 20% of the present world population – over 1,000 million people – and is growing faster than the world population, mainly because the Muslim birth rate is higher.

Eastern religions enslave over 600 million people and have seen something of a resurgence since the fall of communism.

In Europe, twenty-two countries have less than 1% of their people who are evangelical Christians; in eleven of them the number is less than 0.2%.

3. Misease about the censure of the world

There has been, particularly in recent years, a fierce onslaught on the Christian mission force, accusing it of destroying foreign cultures and questioning its right to go into all the world and preach the gospel. While missionaries have, undoubtedly, been guilty at times in the past of confusing culture with the gospel, many of the 'cultural' changes brought about have been achieved as a result, both of the persuasion of Christian workers on moral grounds and for the good of the people concerned, and of the power of the gospel working for change from within the hearts of men and women. Often, the opponents of mission would have us believe that arrogant missionaries go into some idyllic paradise or Garden of Eden and try and force on people their own standards and cultures. The truth is that very often the entrance of the gospel has brought with it great social and physical well-being and an end to some of the cruellest pagan practices. The truth is that there is good and bad in all cultures – my own included – and the Christian has a duty and responsibility under God to expose the bad wherever he sees it.

My first experience of Africa – though it's not strictly African at all – was in Madagascar. Here, something in the region of 90% of the population worship their ancestors. On special occasions, the bones of dead parents and relatives are removed from their tombs, washed and wrapped in fresh silk before being paraded around the streets to the accompaniment of loud and lively music. Huge expense is incurred as long parties take place while the bones are reinterred and laid to rest until the next time. When a recent BBC programme showed this gruesome and occult practice, it was praised as a good way of keeping in touch with the past and a good excuse for fun. The truth is that a country which has the natural potential for being quite well off is one of the poorest in the world because it is in constant debt to its dead ancestors and steeped in practices God's Word unequivocally condemns.

The following extract comes from the diary of

William Carey and concerns the practice of Sati which was common in India. On the death of a Brahmin, his wife or wives – on one occasion thirty-three of them – were burned alive on his funeral pyre. Carey fought against this for years and was instrumental in its being outlawed.

'We saw a number of people assembled on the river-side. I asked for what they were met, and they told me to burn the body of a dead man. I enquired if his wife would die with him: they answered yes, and pointed to her. She was standing by the pile of large billets of wood, on the top of which lay her husband's dead body. Her nearest relative stood by her; and near her was a casket of sweetmeats. I asked if this was her choice, or if she were brought to it by any improper influence. They answered that it was perfectly voluntary. I talked till reasoning was of no use, and then began to exclaim with all my might against what they were doing, telling them it was shocking murder.

'They told me it was a great act of holiness, and added in a very surly manner, that, if I did not like to see it, I might go further off, and desired me to do so. I said I would not go, that I was determined to stay and see the murder, against which I should certainly bear witness at the tribunal of God. I exhorted the widow not to throw away her life; to fear nothing, for no evil would follow her refusal to be burned. But in the most calm manner she mounted the pile and danced on it with her hands extended, as if in the utmost tranquillity of spirit. Previous to this, the relative, whose office it was to set fire to the pile, led her six times round it – thrice at a time. As she went round, she scattered the sweetmeats amongst the people, who ate them as a very holy thing. This being ended, she lay down beside the corpse, and put one arm under its neck and the other over it, then a quantity of dry cocoa-leaves and other substances were heaped over them to a considerable height, and then ghi (oil) was poured on the top. Two bamboos were then put over them, and held fast down, and fire put to the pile, which immediately blazed very fiercely, owing to the dry and combustible materials of which it was composed. No sooner was the fire kindled than all the people set up a great shout of joy, invoking Siva. It was impossible to have heard the woman, had she groaned, or even cried aloud, on account of the shoutings of the people, and again it was impossible for her to stir or struggle, by reason of the bamboos held down on her, like the levers of a press. We made much objection to their use of these, insisting that it was undue force, to prevent her getting up when the fire burned. But they declared it was only to keep the fire from falling down. We could not bear to see more, and left them, exclaiming loudly against the murder, and filled with horror at what we had seen.'[13]

Here is a testimony, again from India, of a converted Brahmin priest, speaking to lepers in an asylum.

'Brothers, you owe much to the Lord Jesus. Here you are housed and fed, clothed and cared for by those who are his followers. How different was your condition under Brahmin rule! At my village of Bisarna, whose priest I was, a leper was once brought to me, and the villagers asked me what they should do with him. I replied, "Dig his grave and bury him." Under my instructions the grave was dug, and the leper was forced into it, where he was buried alive.'

Such 'cultural interference' was prompted by a desire for the glory of God and the well-being of men and women who were, as in Jesus' day, 'harassed and helpless, like sheep without a shepherd'.

4. Misrepresentation of the character of mission work
Mission appears to mean different things to different people today. It would, perhaps, be helpful at this stage to clearly define what mission is or is not.

Mission is evangelism
The church of Christ, like her Lord, must be sensitive to the hunger, poverty and suffering in the world and be involved in sacrificial service to the needy world around. But such service by itself will not be

fulfilling the mission of the church. It is right and proper that Christians are, as they often have been, at the forefront of efforts to alleviate suffering and improve people's conditions – and how often God has used these to open doors for the gospel and build bridgeheads into previously unreached communities – but to leave it at that level is not sufficient. John Stott has strongly argued for this equal partnership position and goes so far to say, 'neither is a means to the other, or even a manifestation of the other. For each is an end in itself.'[14] However, the Bible clearly teaches that evangelism is not an equal partner with social concern but affirms the primacy of the spiritual over the physical. The message of the gospel is primarily redemptive not humanitarian and there needs to be, wherever the opportunity arises, the verbal proclamation of the Good News of salvation without which men and women cannot be saved.

The Lausanne Covenant puts it like this: 'in the church's mission of sacrificial service, *evangelism is primary*. World evangelisation requires the whole church to take the whole gospel (including compassion and practical care) to the whole world' (italics mine).

In my travels around the country in recent years, I have met two serving and godly ministers who had been turned down by two different mainline mission agencies on the grounds that they were 'only Bible teachers' and therefore had nothing to offer to overseas mission work. Incidentally, these are not agencies working in countries which are closed to normal missionary methods. They were told that had they been joiners, brain surgeons or mechanics there was plenty of work for them to do, but what good are preachers and Bible teachers to missionary societies today? It's a tragic reflection on and indictment of the church here in the West that we no longer see the need of communicating the gospel to other cultures and are satisfied with alleviating suffering and meeting material needs.

To many today mission is no longer first and foremost about the proclamation of the good news of the gospel, the storming of Satan's kingdom and the rescuing of precious souls. The material needs of men and women have taken precedence over the spiritual, matters temporal over matters eternal. People are moved by haunting pictures of African children with distended bellies or rat-infested shanty towns and will respond generously with their giving. But where is the same tugging of the heart strings for the unseen but even greater spiritual plight in which millions still exist today? Jesus' response to the needs of the people of his day, seeing them 'as sheep without a shepherd', was 'teaching them many things'.

Personally, I am grateful and privileged to be on the home staff of a society that places a great emphasis on the centrality of preaching and teaching in the work of mission and has as its two main aims, the evangelising of the unreached and the training of national leaders.

Dick Dowsett of OMF has got the balance right. 'Jesus was clear that his priority was bringing people to eternal life. Everything took second place to the preaching of the gospel, to the sharing the Good News, therefore this must be the church's priority too.'[15]

When it gets its act together, the world can do a pretty good job of clothing, feeding and healing people, but the Christian church has a message the world knows nothing about and cares little for, a message that can touch men and women at a far deeper and more critical point of need. If *all* we do is meet people's physical needs then we actually do them a disservice; improving and prolonging this life but failing to warn them of the necessity to prepare for eternity.

Mission is cross-cultural

Many believe that it is enough if we engage in evangelism in our neighbourhood and the community in which we live. But the Bible brings such words as *all nations*, *the whole creation*, *the world*, *the ends of the earth* to our attention. Neither did the Lord say to his disciples that they should complete the evangelisation of Jerusalem and then move on to Judea and Samaria and then to the ends of the earth. It is Jerusalem *and* Judea *and* Samaria *and* the ends of the earth. Mission in many churches is local mission and no more than that, but a church that has no concern for cross-cultural evangelism is not fulfilling its God-given commission.

Mission is church planting

Jesus said, 'I will build my church' (Matt. 16:18) and this must always be the chief task of mission. While Jesus was speaking about 'the church universal', the disciples took up the work by planting local churches wherever they went. You cannot read the Book of Acts without realising that this was Paul's strategy. Wherever he or the other apostles went they sought to establish churches, and when they had done so, and organised them, they moved on elsewhere to start again. The mission of the church does not end with the mere proclamation of the gospel. The Great Commission, as we shall see more fully in a later study, places on the church the duty of making 'disciples', who are those who are taught 'to obey everything I have commanded you'.

This means that there must be the establishing of communities of worshipping men and women, the planting of churches in places where there is no church. Until this has been achieved we have no warrant for saying that a people have been 'discipled'.

Notes

1. John R W Stott, article in *Perspectives on the World Christian Movement* (William Carey Library) p. 3.

2. Hywel R Jones, *Only One Way* (Day One Publications) p.136.

3. John R W Stott, *op. cit.* p. 4.

4. Peter Beyerhaus, *Shaken Foundations: Theological Foundations for Missions* (Zondervan) pp. 41-42.

5. Quoted in Tom Wells, *A Vision for Missions* (Banner of Truth) p. 123.

6. Glen Myers, *The World Christian Starter Kit* (WEC/STL) p.13.

7. Edmund Clowney, *Preaching and Biblical Theology*, p. 69.

8. Paul Borthwick, *A Mind for Missions* (NavPress) p. 34.

9. Ruth A Tucker, *From Jerusalem to Irian Jaya*, (Zondervan) p. 115.

10. Martin Goldsmith, *Don't Just Stand There*, (IVP) p. 8.

11. David Howard, quoted by Paul Borthwick, *A Mind for Missions*, (NavPress) p. 24.

12. John Piper, *Let the Nations be Glad*, (IVP) p. 44.

13. Quoted in S Pearce Carey, *William Carey*, (Hodder and Stoughton) pp. 176-177.

14. John Stott, *Christian Mission in the Modern World*, (Falcon) p. 27.

15. Dick Dowsett, *God, That's Not Fair!* (OMF/STL) p. 63.

2

HIS STORY

The Story of Mission

At the close of his earthly life and ministry, Jesus gave his disciples authority to evangelise the world in his name and promised them the power of the Holy Spirit to do the work. At Pentecost, the Christians received that power and were thrust out into the world to tell the good news, and their obedience to Jesus' commission is faithfully recorded in the New Testament. We take up the story when the last surviving apostle, John, had died in about AD 97.

100-500 – Rapid advance

Eusebius, the historian, describes the early Christians in this way: 'At the time [about the beginning of the second century] many Christians felt their souls inspired by the holy Word with a passionate desire for perfection. Their first action, in obedience to the instructions of the Saviour, was to sell their goods and to distribute them to the poor. Then, leaving their homes, they set out to fulfil the work of an evangelist, making it their ambition to preach the Word of the faith to those who as yet had heard nothing of it, and to commit to them the books of the divine gospels. They were content simply to lay the foundations of the faith among those foreign peoples: they then appointed other pastors and committed to them the responsibility for building up those whom they had merely brought to the faith. Then they passed on to other countries and nations with the grace and help of God.'

By 150, Justin Martyr, the Christian apologist, could say: 'There is not one single race of men, whether barbarians or Greeks, or whatever they may be called, nomads, or vagrants, or herdsmen dwelling in tents, among whom prayers and giving of thanks are not offered through the name of the crucified Jesus.' This is clearly a gross overstatement of the facts yet it indicates the impression that was given by this rapid advance of the message of the gospel. Indeed Pliny, the Roman Governor of Bithynia, what we now know as north east Turkey, reported in 111 that Christianity had gained such a hold upon the people that the heathen temples were almost empty.

However, it has to be said that, while the spread of the gospel was rapid overall, its progress was far from even. It took hold most firmly in Syria where, by the end of the fourth century, half of the population of half a million professed faith; in Rome where the church was predominantly made up of the 'lower classes', and in North Africa.

What, from a human perspective, were the reasons for such dramatic progress? The following reasons have been suggested:

Persuasion

There was a burning conviction among the early Christians that the lost must be reached with the gospel, and that they, as believers, were called to do the work. We have already seen this in the comments made by Eusebius.

Purity of life

In those days, to be a Christian really meant something. It was, by and large, a day of very lax morals, and the very high standard among the Christians was a great witness to others.

Practice of love

Even the apostate Emperor Julian had to admit that 'Atheism (by which he meant the Christian faith) has been specially advanced through the loving sacrifice rendered to strangers, and through their care for the burial of the dead. It is a scandal that there is not a single Jew who is a beggar, and that the godless Galileans care not only for their poor, but for ours as well; while those who belong to us look in vain for the help that we render them.

Persecution

A great impression was made by the dignity of those killed for their faith as these cameos of Ignatius and Polycarp reveal.

Ignatius was Bishop of the church in Antioch for forty years. When an old man, he was brought before the Emperor, Trajan.

Trajan: 'There you are, wicked devil, deceiver of men!'

Ignatius: 'Not an evil spirit, but I have Jesus Christ in my heart.'

Trajan: 'Jesus Christ within you? Do you mean him who was crucified by Pontius Pilate?'

Ignatius: 'Yes, he was crucified for my sins.'

Without any further legal proceedings, Ignatius was ordered to be transferred to Rome and thrown to the wild beasts. He said, 'I thank thee, O Lord, that thou hast vouchsafed thus to honour me....I am God's grain, to be ground between the teeth of wild beasts, so that I may become a holy loaf for the Lord.'

At the age of eighty-six, *Polycarp* was betrayed and handed over to his enemies. He was required on oath to call Caesar 'Lord' as if he were divine. Polycarp's refusal was firm. 'I have wild beasts,' said the consul. 'If you will not change your mind I will throw you to them.' Polycarp replied, 'Bid them be brought.' 'If you despise the beasts, unless you change your mind, I shall have you burnt,' retorted the consul. 'Swear and I release you; curse Christ.'

'Eighty-six years have I served him,' replied the old man, 'and he has done me no wrong; how then can I blaspheme my King who saved me? You threaten the fire that burns for an hour, and after a little while is quenched; for you are ignorant of the fire of judgement to come, and of everlasting punishment reserved for the ungodly. But why delay? Do what you wish.'

As the smoke and flame encircled him, he prayed, 'Lord God, Father of our blessed Saviour, I thank thee that I have been deemed worthy to receive the crown of martyrdom, and that I may die for thee and for thy cause.'

500-1500 – Religious superstition

Nonetheless, the advance of the gospel was so successful that, by the time of the conversion of the Emperor Constantine, much of the Roman Empire was already largely, at least nominally, Christian. Sadly, the very popularity of Christianity hastened its spiritual decline and departure from a biblical faith. With Constantine's 'Edict of Milan' in 313, Christianity became the state religion of the Roman Empire and people flooded to the church in great numbers. As a result, there seemed little need of missionary effort as thousands were entering the church, but individual conversions and personal commitment were no longer of great concern.

Then a militant religion erupted out of the Arabian deserts and spread into the heartlands of the Christian world. Islam became a scourge for the church that had become increasingly inward focused. Mohammed was born in 570 and experienced his first visions and messages around 610. By the time of his death, twenty-two years later, he had released a flood that quickly engulfed most of the Christian lands, and only remnants of the once strong church survived. By 700, Muslim armies had reached the Atlantic and penetrated deep into Western Europe,

Central Asia and India. This wide arc of territory restricted Christianity to a section of Europe – where the influence of the gospel spread quite rapidly – and for 1,000 years prevented major missionary advance.

The Christian response to Islam was hardly biblical. The church tried to break down this force by the means of eight Crusades which ran from the time of the initial capture of Jerusalem in 1099 to the final loss of the last Crusader stronghold in 1291. This military backlash was a tragic mistake and immeasurably damaged the cause of Christ among Muslim peoples. Even today, the typical villain in Muslim eyes is an armour-clad soldier with a cross on his shield.

There were, however, some windows of opportunity which should not be overlooked:

Columba (521-597)
By 500, the church in Britain, which had been established in the second or third century, had withdrawn almost entirely into Wales. In 563, Columba, an Irishman, crossed to the island of Iona, off the west coast of Scotland, and founded a number of monasteries in Scotland before his death thirty-four years later.

Wynfrith of Crediton – Boniface (c680-754)
Described as 'a man who had a deeper influence on the history of Europe than any Englishman who has ever lived'[1], Boniface was a man gifted with great

organisational skills as well as fired by a passionate conviction of the necessity of preaching the gospel of Christ. His main work was among the Germanic tribes of Gaul and he brought over many missionaries from his home land to assist him in the work of evangelisation. He was murdered during yet another missionary expedition while in his seventies.

Francis of Assisi (1182-1226)
This saintly man caught a glimpse of the missionary heart of God. In an age when so much of the church was throwing her energies into putting Muslims to the sword, Francis made three separate attempts to reach these same Muslims with the gospel of peace, visiting Morocco, Spain and Egypt as an ambassador for Christ. His efforts made little impact though.

Ramon Lull (1235-1315)
Described by Stephen Neill as 'one of the greatest missionaries in the history of the Church'[2], Lull, who was born on the island of Majorca, was confronted by Islam to the west and south, in Spain and North Africa. He founded a missionary training school and language centre in Majorca and devoted the last fifty years of his life to missionary endeavour. He wrote, 'Missionaries will convert the world by preaching, but also through the shedding of tears and with great labour, and through bitter death.' He himself paid that ultimate price after preaching the gospel to a crowd of angry Muslims in North Africa.

Peter Waldo (-1217)

Waldo was a successful merchant banker, living in the French city of Lyons early in the twelfth century. He was converted in 1175, having been made to think seriously about eternal matters following the death of a guest at a dinner party. By this time the Bible had already been translated into his local dialect, and it was through reading Matthew 19:21, that Peter Waldo decided to sell everything he owned and become an itinerant preacher. Soon a group gathered around him and they became known as 'the poor men of Lyons'. Travelling in pairs they carried the good news of Christ across France and into Italy and Austria.

Waldo became a catalyst for many people who had already founded their faith and practice on the Scriptures, and also others who, through preaching, had believed in Christ. One such group lived in the Alpine valleys of northern Italy and, inspired by the example of Waldo, they began to reach out to other areas with the gospel. The Waldensians, as they were to become known, were renowned for their love of the Scriptures and many learned parts of the New Testament and Psalms by heart. A Bible College was established and missionaries were trained and then sent out as pedlars and merchants with the purpose of reaching men and women for Christ.

Inevitably, the Church of Rome was quickly stirred into action against this movement and Waldo himself was excommunicated in 1184, after refusing to recant. Five hundred of his followers were arrested in Strasbourg in 1212 and eighty of them were burned at the stake. In the years following Waldo's own death in 1217, thousands of Waldensians were murdered, including many women and children, and by 1400 the persecutions had reached such a point that many fled to the high mountain regions of northern Italy, though, even here they did not escape. On one terrible occasion four hundred women and children were discovered hiding in a cave. The entrance was sealed and everyone inside was left to die. However, the Waldensian preachers travelled great distances across Europe and at one time, so it was said, a preacher could travel from Cologne to Florence and stay every night in the home of a believer. By the end of the sixteenth century, it was claimed that Protestants in the Piedmont valley outnumbered the Catholics in the proportion of 100 to 1. The Waldensian Church still exists in Italy to this day but sadly it has lost its evangelical fire and is now liberal.

Summary

Perhaps the most distressing aspect of this period of the church's history, is that the pure gospel of God, enshrined in the inspired Scriptures, was submerged by religious attitudes and inventions which can only be described as demonic. There was very little missionary enterprise as Christianity, almost buried by religious superstition, tradition and ignorance, busied itself building cathedrals and monasteries. The light was never completely lost, though, since

43

God always keeps a remnant of faithful people who refuse to bow the knee to Baal. There were, even as we have seen, lights in this dark time, voices of concern and protest; but the Reformation was to come like a mighty light, breaking into these dark ages, and when true believers combined a mission strategy with rediscovered evangelical theology, they began to raise an army of missionaries, the like of which had not been seen for centuries.

1500-1700 – Reformed theology

By the end of these 'Dark Ages', much of Christianity had become enshrouded in superstition and false teaching and Islam was more firmly entrenched than ever across many nations.

However, the Reformation came like a mighty light, breaking into the darkness of spiritual ignorance. Men like Luther, Calvin and Knox began to speak out against the idolatry, corruption and false teaching of the Roman Church and looked to the Bible as the sole authority for the true Christian.

Our main interest lies in the effect of the Reformation on the church's response to the Lord's Great Commission. It was, essentially, two-fold:

(1) the Reformation restored to the church the great truths of personal salvation through Christ, and, eventually, this newly rediscovered evangelical theology gave fresh impetus to the cause of world mission;

(2) the Reformation coincided with the invention of the new printing technology in Germany which

produced a revolution in communications. By the year 1500, six million books had been printed in Europe. This was vital to the Reformation because it brought the Bible to the fore and made it available to the masses. Later it helped spread the teachings of the Reformers through the many books and tracts they were to write.

During the sixteenth and seventeenth centuries, the all-consuming challenge for the church was to put her own house in order, and it was, in many ways, a period of dynamic 'home mission' for the Protestants. But that does not mean to say that there was no missionary activity going on.

Here is just one example of the sort of missionary enterprise that was taking place at this time. One writer depicts a travelling preacher going from town to town, preaching, teaching and selling Reformed literature.

'In Switzerland, I and my books have met with more sudden and violent varieties of reception than anywhere else – the people are so free and unrestrained. In some villages, the chief men, or the priest himself, summoned all the inhabitants by the church bell to hear all that I had to tell.... In other villages on the contrary, the peasants gathered angrily around me, reviled me as a spy and an intruding foreigner, and drove me with stones and rough jousts from among them, threatening that I should not escape so easily another time.

'In some places they have advanced much further than among us in Germany. The images have been removed from their churches, and the service is read in the language of the people.

'But the great joy is to see the light that has not been spread only from torch to torch, as human illuminations spread, but has burst at once upon Germany, France and Switzerland, as heavenly light dawns from above.'

1700-1900 – Renewed Vision

It was at the turn of the seventeenth century that world mission was once again taken up with renewed vigour by the Reformed church. In 1701, 'The Society for the Propagation of the Gospel in Foreign Parts' was founded, the first Anglican missionary society. They made sporadic attempts to propagate the gospel among the unreached of America, the West Indies and West Africa, but without much success. Underlying the failure lay a lack of real commitment and vision for those outside the church and, ultimately, a lack of resources.

Let's take a look at just a few of the remarkable men of faith who were obedient to the Great Commission during these years.

Count Zinzendorf (1700-1760)

At Halle University, a boarding school, there was a young student, an aristocrat, with a growing desire for the world to hear the gospel. Count Nicolas Ludwig von Zinzendorf has been described 'the first in modern times on whose heart lay day and night the desire that all the ends of the earth might see the salvation of God'.

In 1724, Zinzendorf founded a community of persecuted refugees in Moravia, calling it 'Herrnhut', meaning 'Lord's Watch'. His intention was that it should be a place where living Christianity could be extended to the whole world through two means – renewal to the existing church and outreach to the unreached.

The first two or three years of its existence were characterised by squabbles and dissensions, until Zinzendorf and three others committed themselves to pray for the whole community. Before long, the tide turned and bitterness and prejudice were replaced by deep repentance and love. One momentous day in August 1727, as the community was celebrating the Lord's Supper, the Holy Spirit came on the gathering and a great revival began that was to touch many corners of the world. The little Herrnhut community adopted an ambitious world-wide strategy and in the last twenty years of Zinzendorf's life sent out 226 members to overseas work, achieving more in world mission than all the Protestant churches together had accomplished in the previous 200 years. Over a period of 150 years, 2,000 of the community's members were sent out as missionaries of the gospel. One in sixty of these Moravian Christians became missionaries – at one point the ratio of missionaries to members reached one in twelve! – compared with one in five thousand in the rest of Protestantism.

In 1727, Moravian missionaries were sent to the West Indies; in 1733 to Greenland; in 1734 to the

American Indians; in 1735 to Surinam and in 1736 to South Africa. This was a fantastic achievement, with nobodies meeting impossibilities and seeing miracles. The first two missionaries walked to their ship at Copenhagen because they had no money available for the overland trip from Moravia.

After the 'Moravian Pentecost', a prayer vigil was started. Each hour of the day was allotted to one of twenty-four praying pairs, so that day after day, night after night, for over 100 years, a continual flow of prayer for world evangelisation and revival ascended to God. There followed a great spiritual awakening on both sides of the Atlantic which lasted throughout the century under John Wesley, George Whitefield and others, and thousands of new converts were gathered into praying congregations. In 1724, a 'Concert of Prayer' was called by Scottish ministers in Cambuslang, with special meetings for revival and evangelism. The call was also taken up by Jonathan Edwards in America.

William Carey (1761-1834)
One of these concerts of prayer was held in Kettering, Northants, where one of the leading lights was William Carey, a shoemaker and Strict Baptist pastor. From boyhood he had been fascinated by the wider world and, on his conversion, God used this to burden his heart for the unreached of the nations. He gathered as much information as he could on the religious state of the world and plotted it on a large leather map in his workshop.

In 1792, Carey wrote a treatise called *An Enquiry into the Obligations of Christians to use Means for the Conversion of the Heathen* in which he battled against the hyper-Calvinism of the day, arguing that 'if Moravians could send out missionaries – why not Strict Baptists?' His fellow-clergy seemed less keen than Carey, but he kept putting 'the evangelisation of the heathen' on the agenda of their fraternals. At their meeting in May 1792, Carey preached a sermon from Isaiah 54:2-3 and cried, 'Expect great things, attempt great things.' The well known additional words, 'from God' and 'for God' allegedly did not appear until some twenty-five years later. His pamphlet on the state of the world, highlighting the fact that seven-ninths of the world population was still unreached, was discussed at the next day's business session, but was met with the usual unsympathetic response. Carey, turning to one of his colleagues, Andrew Fuller, gripped his arm and exclaimed, 'Is nothing again going to be done, sir?' Fuller suddenly reconsidered and was converted to the cause and the others followed. Four months later the Baptist Missionary Society was formed and, in June 1793, Carey and his family, left for India, never to return.

Carey's mission policy was based on five main principles:

1. the widespread preaching of the gospel by every possible method;
2. support of the preaching by the distribution of Bibles in the language of the country;

3. the establishment, at the earliest opportunity, of a church;
4. a profound study of the background and thought of the non-Christian people;
5. training, at the earliest possible moment, of an indigenous ministry.

Though he waited nearly seven years for his first convert, and suffered enormous set-back and difficulties, Carey achieved notable success in each of these areas. On one occasion a dreadful fire destroyed the results of many months of translation work in several languages, yet they set to with a believing determination to rebuild and renew their efforts. His achievements in Bible translation alone are remarkable and noteworthy. He translated the whole Bible into six languages; the New Testament and part of the Old into another five; the New Testament into five more; and one or more of the Gospels into yet another five. In all, thirty-four languages received all or part of the Scriptures as a result of Carey's ministry.

Carey's emphasis was on organised effort in the form of missionary societies and this was essential to the success of the missionary enterprise. In the first twenty-five years after Carey sailed for India, twelve missionary societies were formed, and by the end of the 1800s, every nominally Christian country, and almost every denomination, had begun to play its part. The 'Haystack Prayer Meeting' in America was begun by a group of college students who were stirred by Carey's *Enquiry*, and led to a vibrant and fruitful student mission movement. These were years of rapid geographical growth with missionaries reaching Japan, Korea, China, South East Asia, the Muslim world and the African Interior.

Robert Morrison (1782-1834)

In 1807, Robert Morrison went with the London Missionary Society as the first Protestant missionary to China. He was unable to find passage on a British ship and was forced to sail to China via the USA. As he was being booked on board, he was asked by the ship's owner, 'And so, Mr. Morrison, you really expect to make an impression on the idolatry of the great Chinese Empire?' To which Morrison replied, 'No, sir, I expect God will.' His labours were neither spectacular nor encouraging; he ministered patiently at Canton for ten years without seeing a single convert. At the same time he diligently worked on a careful translation of the Bible into Chinese, completing the New Testament in 1814 and the Old Testament in 1819. Working alone for much of the time and enduring much opposition and privation, Morrison paved the way for the tide of church workers who poured into China later in the nineteenth century.

Adoniram Judson (1788-1850)

The first American overseas missionary, Judson left for Burma in 1813 and served for thirty-five years with scarcely a break. He mastered the Burmese language and script, translating and revising the Burmese New Testament and Bible, and preaching regularly. He worked for five years before he saw his first convert and during the Anglo-Burmese war was kept for eighteen months in a squalid prison as a suspected spy.

David Livingstone (1813-1873)

Inspired by his meeting with Dr. Robert Moffatt, who was a missionary to Africa and was to become his father-in-law, Dr. David Livingstone set sail for Africa in 1840. Penetrating the previously unexplored heartland of this vast continent, Livingstone constantly fought against the slave trade, opening up new and better routes into Central Africa. Though remembered today primarily as a great explorer and geographer, he never lost sight of his mission. 'I am a missionary, heart and soul,' he once said, 'God had only one son and he was a missionary and physician. A poor, poor imitation of him I am, or wish to be. In his service I hope to live, in it I wish to die.'

Hudson Taylor (1832-1905)

Hudson Taylor, a Yorkshireman, realised that all existing mission agencies were confined to the coastland areas of continents like Africa and Asia. Having spent a few years in China under the auspices of the Chinese Evangelisation Society, Taylor parted company with them over their financial policy, and returned to England where, in 1865, he formed a new society, the China Inland Mission, praying that God would raise up twenty-four missionaries for China – two for each of the eleven unoccupied provinces, and two more for Chinese Tartary. Workers came from different denominations, and were readily accepted provided that they held to the full inspiration of Scripture, looked only to God for the provision of their needs – no appeals being made for money, would be prepared to wear Chinese dress and to go inland. By 1870, the number of missionaries stood at thirty-three and rose to well over 1,000 by the end of the century.

Taylor's emphasis on the heartlands and unreached interiors of various parts of the world, allied with his unshakeable commitment to the faith principle, saw the birth of what Ralph Winter calls 'The Second Era' of modern missions.[3] Soon after the founding of the China Inland Mission (now OMF), came Sudan Interior Mission (now Action Partners), Africa Inland Mission, Unevangelised Fields Mission and many others.

Peter Cameron Scott (1867-1896)

At the age of twenty-three, Scott set sail for Africa as a missionary. Two years later he was carried unconscious with fever on to a ship back to England. In 1895, at the age of twenty-nine, he set off again, with seven other recruits, bound for East Africa. They headed inland for two months travelling on foot. During that first year, Scott walked 2,600 miles before dying of blackwater fever, but by then four mission stations had been established and through him the Africa Inland Mission had been born.

AD1900 – Remarkable progress
When, in 1920, the World Missions Conference convened in Edinburgh with 1,200 delegates, they reviewed the work of the previous 100 years, revealing a remarkable achievement. Less than 120 years after Carey had sailed for India and launched the greatest missionary awakening, from a position when seven-ninths of the world's population was unreached, now about half of the world's 1,625 million people were, in some sense, within range of Christian influence. A fantastic dream had become a reality.

However, Glen Myers points to three main problems:

1. 'Christianity, though world-wide, was just a token presence in most countries. Only about one and a quarter million non-Westerners had become Protestant church members; four or five times that number were probably attending the churches.

2. 'The "native" Christians were often misfits and outcasts from their own societies. Converts had tended to draw away from their own people and form new communities based around the mission compound; in that way the gospel was actually depleting tribes rather than blessing them.

3. 'Almost universally, the missionaries were in sole charge of the churches they founded. Few yet realised the biblical principle of partnership between the old churches and new for world evangelisation. The Westerners were in control and the church was unbalanced.'[4]

During this twentieth century, God has, by his Spirit, been moving in quite astonishing ways throughout the world, bringing the glorious message of salvation to more and more people and bringing many of them into his kingdom. More people have been swept into the church during this century than in all the revivals throughout previous history. In 1900 there were some 72,000,000 evangelicals world-wide. By 1985 that figure had risen to 255,000,000, more than 3½ times as many, with the greatest growth being in Asia, Latin America and Africa. Let's consider some of the highlights of this exciting period in mission history and then take a look at some of the remarkable changes that have taken place in different parts of the world.

Student Volunteer Movement for Foreign Missions
The closing years of the nineteenth century saw the rise of a movement which inspired more than 100,000 students to volunteer for mission service. Described as 'history's single most potent mission organization' 20,000 actually went overseas while the remainder strengthened the necessary homebase.

The Hidden Peoples

In 1934, a new era of missions began, with an effort to reach the 'Hidden Peoples'. Cameron Townsend, a student volunteer from Los Angeles, went to Guatemala, distributing Spanish literature. However, he quickly discovered that the majority of the people didn't understand Spanish. An Indian asked him, 'If your God is so smart, why can't he speak our language?' Townsend formed the Wycliffe Bible Translators in response. At the time it was thought that there were 500 unreached tribal groups in the world, but that figure was later revised upwards, firstly to 1,000, then to 2,000, and is now estimated to be nearer 3,000.

Jim Elliot (1927-1956)

Jim, whose father was a preacher, trusted Christ when he was six and became a fearless witness for his Saviour. As a student he always carried his Bible on top of his school books and, though possessing a great ability in architectural drawing, felt a strong call of God to mission service. While in Bible College he met his future wife, Elisabeth, and spent his holidays in Mexico helping missionaries and becoming convinced that Latin America was where God was directing him. At the age of twenty-five he went, with Elisabeth, to Ecuador to work among the Quichua Indians in the eastern jungles but had a burning desire for the unreached Auca who were savage killers. The Aucas were distrustful of white men because of previous atrocities they had suffered.

After some initial contact with the Aucas, Jim Elliot and his four colleagues landed in the jungle and set up camp. Three days later their bodies were found; they had died from spear and machete wounds.

South Korea

Here, there has been the greatest ingathering in one nation ever known in church history. In 1900 there were just 6,400 evangelicals in the whole of the country. By 1985, that figure had risen by a staggering one thousand fold to 6.4 million. In South Korea today, one Korean in every five is an evangelical believer. All statistics in this country are breathtaking. The first Protestant church was opened in 1884. By 1984 there were 30,000 of them, and there are now 7,000 congregations in Seoul alone, including the world's largest congregation which has a membership of well over 500,000.

China

The Edinburgh Conference in 1910 directed particular attention to China and Patrick Johnstone says that 'The growth of the church in China since 1977 has no parallels in history'.[5]

In 1951 the communist revolution closed the doors to foreign missionaries and great persecution followed. It was estimated that in 1970 there were probably 2,000,000 Christians in China, but by 1992 this figure had risen to 63,000,000. At the present rate of growth, by the end of this century, there will be more people with a living faith in Christ in China than in any other land in the world.

Indonesia

In 1965, a communist coup resulted in 500,000 believers being killed. During the next six years, 2,000,000 from the island of Java alone were baptised. Since 1970, another 20,000,000 believers have been added to the church in Indonesia.

Latin America

In 1900 there were just 2-3,000 evangelicals against a very bigoted and corrupt Roman Catholic church. Then there was a period of fierce persecution when buildings were dynamited, believers martyred and Bibles burned. During this time, there was explosive growth in the Christian church of about 10% a year – so that by 1990 there were 46,000,000 evangelicals, representing 11% of the population, and the figure is expected to rise to 80,000,000 by the end of the century. There are now more evangelicals than Roman Catholics in churches, and in countries such as Brazil, Guatemala, Chile and El Salvador, evangelicals are the major religious force.

Africa

In 1900, there were 2.5 million Protestants in Africa, representing about 10% of the population. There are now some 109 million, making up 23% of the total population. The evangelical community has increased from 1.9% in 1900 to 13.2% in 1990, a seven fold increase in percentage, but an increase of nearly thirty-fold in actual numbers. In the AIM and SIM daughter churches, more worship on a Sunday than in all the churches in Britain put together.

Conclusion

'World Christianity ... is the result of the great missionary expansion of the last two centuries. That expansion, whatever one's attitude to Christianity may be, is one of the most remarkable facts in human history.'[6]

'The Missionary enterprise was and is and will be a work full of human faultlines, errors, limitation and sin .... The fact stands, however, that the awakening since the eighteenth century of the missionary spirit in the church is one of the most amazing movements in the history of the world.'[7]

Certainly, today, the church world-wide is bigger, more active and more expansionary than at any time in history. There are some of God's people in every country on earth. There are more Bibles, more church buildings, more full-time Christian workers, more missionaries and more worship in more languages than ever before.

But there is still much to be done ....

Notes
1. Christopher Dawson, qtd by Stephen Neill, *A History of Christian Missions*, Pelican, p. 74.
2. Stephen Neill, *A History of Christian Missions*, Pelican, p.134.
3. Ralph D Winter, article in *Perspectives on the World Christian Movement*, William Carey Library, p. 172.
4. Glen Myers, *The World Christian Starter Kit* WEC/STL pp. 42-43.
5. Patrick Johnstone, *Operation World (1993)* STL p. 164.
6. Lesslie Newbigin, *Christianity and World Revolution*, ed. E H Rian, Harper and Row, p. 149.
7. Herbert Kraemer, *The Christian Message in the Non-Christian World*, Edinburgh House Press, p. 34.

3

THE UNFINISHED TASK

The Challenge of Mission

So far, in our consideration of *Mission Matters*, we have looked at what God's Word says about world mission – the biblical basis and pattern – and we have seen how the church has, down through the ages, taken up that task, or otherwise. The question we must address at this point is – how well have we done? How far have we got?

In his Great Commission, Jesus gave us three goals by which we can gauge how much the church has done to fulfil the task entrusted to it in that commission.

1. Individuals
'Go into all the world and preach the good news to all creation' (Mark 16:15, NIV). The KJV and NKJV translate this as 'to every creature'.

Here is a clear command to evangelise the individual. Everyone on earth has a right to hear the gospel at least once, and it is our job to give it to them. We are accountable to God until the whole earth is saturated with the preaching of the gospel, by whatever means possible.

2. Nations

'Therefore go and make disciples of all nations' (Matt. 28:19). That seems clear enough, doesn't it? The gospel is to be preached to all the nations of the world.

We have already discovered that there are some of the Lord's people in every country on earth. Does that mean, as some would advocate, that the task of world mission is finally, or at least nearly, accomplished? That is the view of many Christians today and, at first glance, might seem correct.

There are some 230 countries in the world today, and in over 180 of them Christians make up at least 1% of the population. Surely that means that the task is nearly done.

Let's go back to Jesus' words in Matthew 28. The word translated 'nations' is the Greek word 'ethne', meaning ethnic groups. This has been defined as 'a significantly large sociological grouping of individuals who perceive themselves to have a common affinity for one another because of their shared language, religion, ethnicity, residence, occupation, class or caste, situation, etc., or combinations of these.'[1]

This is further clarified for us in Revelation 7:9-10 where we have a much fuller picture of what the Lord envisaged when he commissioned his church with the task of world evangelisation: 'After this I looked and there before me was a great multitude that no-one could count, from every nation (*ethnic*), tribe (*social*) people (*political*) and language

61

(*linguistic*), standing before the throne and in front of the Lamb.'

Now, this gives us a clear and identifiable goal. Included in that great gathering around the throne will be representatives from every ethnic, social, political and linguistic people group in the world. That throws a very different light on the overall picture. There are some 7,000 different known languages spoken in the world, but often one language may be used by more than one people group. If we add up all the languages and distinctive ethnic groups in each country, we are faced with a target figure of just over 12,000.

Let's consider a couple of examples of how this alters our whole concept of looking at the unevangelised of the world.

Chad
One of the larger countries in Africa, Chad is made up of over 180 different and distinct people groups, each with their own identity and culture, and at least 120 different languages. Some of those 180 tribes have viable, indigenous churches established among them, but for someone – or a team – to go from one of the 'reached' tribes to one of the as yet 'unreached' ones would take at least as much long-term, cross-cultural missionary effort as for any missionaries from a foreign country. Yet, Revelation 7 tells us that, among that worshipping crowd in heaven, there will be, not simply a representative from Chad, but believers from each of these 180 people groups.

India

This vast nation is actually an amazing mixture of distinct people groups and languages. There are twenty-two states in India, but each of these contains many ethnic groups. In all, there are more than 2,900 ethnic groups speaking over 1,900 different languages. When people hear that I was brought up in India, I am sometimes asked the question, 'Can you speak Indian?' The fact is that there is no such language, rather 1,900 different ones.

There, then, are two of the goals that Jesus set for the church – individuals and people groups. But there is a third. The Great Commission lays on the church of Jesus Christ the duty, not just to preach the gospel to, or evangelise, individuals and peoples but to 'make disciples' of them. In the Scriptures, a disciple is never someone who has simply heard the message of the gospel or even made a response to it. A disciple is, in New Testament terms, a baptised, worshipping member of a local community of believers. This means that the third goal of the Great Commission is to establish indigenous communities of baptised, worshipping believers, in each of the people groups of the world, each led by, and reaching out to, their own people.

Let me give you my own paraphrase of Matthew 28:19:

> 'Go and establish indigenous communities of baptised, worshipping, evangelising believers in all ethnic, social, political and linguistic people groups.'

Granted, it's not as memorable as Jesus' own words, but it helps to bring out the force of exactly what Jesus wants his church to do.

So, there are three goals – individuals, people groups and communities of believers. Two of those goals, the last two, are measurable ones and enable us to see just how far the church has got in this task over the last 2,000 years, and immediately we can see that we have little cause for complacency or self-congratulation.

I said earlier that there were about 230 countries in the world today. The number of people groups is estimated to be about 12,000. How many have been 'discipled' or 'reached'?

Of the 12,000 people groups in the world, 6,000 of them are defined as 'majority Christian', though the interpretation of 'Christian' is very wide, and often means no more than nominal. 3,000 of the groups have some viable, indigenous churches within the culture and there is some mission activity among a further 2,000 peoples, though, as yet, no real breakthrough. In the remaining 1,000 there is little or no mission activity, and no indigenous churches. That represents at least one quarter of the peoples of the world that are still largely 'unreached'.

Even then, we must look more closely at the facts. In Europe, for example, where the population is about 515 million, over 77% would claim to be Christian and yet only a tenth are regular church-goers and less than 3% are evangelicals. In several countries within Europe, there are large communities where there is no possibility of hearing the gospel, and we might define them as unreached. In France and Spain less than 1% are evangelicals; in Belgium less that 0.5%, and in Greece less than 0.2%. As Patrick Johnstone says, 'Great swathes of Europe are truly post-Christian with a small "irrelevant", committed Christian remnant, and need to be evangelised again – for example, North Germany, parts of Sweden, rural England and Wales and much of France. Many of these areas have not had much meaningful exposure to biblical Christianity for several generations.'[2]

That figure of one quarter of the peoples of the world is made even more realistic when we realise that it represents between 35 and 40% of the population of the world, and many of them are enslaved by the world's dominant religious blocs – Islam, Hinduism and Buddhism. About a quarter of the present population is beyond the reach of the present proclamation of the gospel.

Let's take a look at a few geographical areas where the need is still great.

The Middle East

There are over 1,035 million Muslims in the world, many of them living in the Middle East, the least evangelised area of the world, with 164 million Arabs, 21.2 million Kurds and 4.5 million Jews.

Few Muslims have ever become Christians, and yet, over the last two or three decades, a growing number have turned to Christ; surely the first fruits of a plentiful harvest that will be won for the Lord. In Saudi Arabia, the focal point of Islam, there is no indigenous Christian church.

Africa

The growth of the church in Africa has, as we have already seen, been amazing. There are 48,000,000 adherents to the church and over 13,000,000 evangelicals, but the task of church planting is by no means over. There are still over 1,000 people groups without a viable church in their culture; Islam claims more than 25% of the population, particularly in the north, and is the greatest challenge to be faced by the church. Of those 180 distinct people groups in Chad that we looked at, nearly 120 of them are still without a Christian witness and a viable, indigenous church.

Asia

There are vast groups of people here without Christ. Over one half of the world's population lives in Asia, in 2,658 people groups, and well over half of these groups are among the least evangelised peoples of the world. Here live 713,000,000 Hindus, 609,000,000 Buddhists, 527,000,000 Muslims and 57,000,000 Animists, most of whom have never heard the gospel.

Hinduism, with its caste system, remains a stronghold to be taken for the gospel. Each of the 3,000 castes is a separate cultural unit, and only from a few dozen of these castes has there been a significant response to the gospel.

The 10/40 Window

Today a lot of attention is being paid by mission agencies to 'The 10/40 Window' – a belt of countries extending from 10 degrees north to 40 degrees north of the equator. Within this area, stretching across North Africa, the Middle East, India and Asia, lives 97% of the population of the least evangelised countries of the world. Here are millions of unreached men and women who may live an entire lifetime without ever hearing about Jesus Christ.

Bible Translation

Before we leave this subject, let's just note the progress that has been made in Bible translation. There are around 7,000 languages spoken in the world. It is sobering to realise that of these, only 355 have the complete Bible, 880 have the New Testament, and 932 have some smaller portion of the Scriptures. That means that about 5,000 – more than half of the languages of the world – have no part of God's Word.[3]

The Remaining Challenge

If the church's task is to establish indigenous churches within each of the 12,000 people groups of the world, the task is far from over. 2,000 years after the giving of that Great Commission, there is still a vast amount of work to be done. Most of the languages of the world are without any or most of God's Word and great swathes of the world's population remain untouched and unreached by the gospel.

Before we think about what our response should

be to these great needs, let's just see what is being done to bring nearer the completion of the task.

There are, today, nearly 140,000 Protestant missionaries in the world. However, the vast majority of the West's contribution to that force, 93-95%, are working with the reached peoples and among existing churches, leaving only a comparative handful to reach, a not only large, but particularly resistant number of people with the gospel. One very real encouragement is the fact that the rising number of Third World missionaries – and it is expected that by the end of the twentieth century they will outnumber those from the West – are concentrating on the unreached and doing church planting. Some 89% of them are working in these areas.

One of the interesting – and exciting – features of this great movement of God over these past one hundred years or so has been the shift in balance between East and West – North America, Europe and the Pacific. In the early sixties, the East had half as many evangelicals as the West. During the late seventies, it had an equal number. By the late eighties, there were twice as many. By 2010, if present trends continue, there could be three times as many non-Western evangelicals as Western.

Evangelicals in the West have, since 1960, experienced an average annual growth of 1.7 % per year. In the rest of the world the 1960 total of 29 million evangelicals grew to 208 million in 1990 – an average annual growth rate of 6.8%.

The imbalance of priorities can also be seen in

the fact that, of all its resources, out of every £1,000 that the church in the West spends, £999 is spent on the Christian world, ninety pence on the evangelised non-Christian world, and just ten pence on the unevangelised.[4]

We have, clearly, still got a long way to go before the vision of Revelation 7:9-10 becomes a reality. I had the enormous privilege of being brought up in a Christian family and have spent most of my life in a country with, perhaps, an unequalled heritage in Christian truth and tradition, and I find it very hard to put myself in the place of someone living all their days in a country, tribe or community where there is no knowledge of the good news of the gospel, no access to Christian things and no opportunity to hear of Christ, and yet that is the situation facing about one in four of the present population of the world.

I often hear people say that most, if not all people have had the chance to hear the gospel; that there is no need for pioneer mission work today as there was, for example, in the days of the apostle Paul and the early church. The truth is that there are ten times as many people needing to hear of Christ for the first time than there were in Paul's day, and the need for pioneer missionaries is therefore ten times greater.

Each one of us who shares the Lord's concern for the lost of the world needs to search our hearts and re-examine our priorities and commitments so that we play our full part in the great work of reaching every nation, tribe, people and language with the glorious news of the gospel.

Notes

1. Edward R. Dayton, *'To reach the Unreached'* article in *Perspectives on the World Christian Movement,* William Carey Library p. 586.
2. Patrick Johnstone, *Operation World* (1993) STL p. 60.
3. SIL Ethnologue (13th Edition).
4. David Barrett, *Seven Hundred Plans to Evangelise the World.*

4

WHO? ME?

The Response to Mission

What is my response going to be? If we are biblical Christians, we can't just look at these things in a detached, academic way. We must personally respond.

The Bible lays before us at least three things we ought to do.

1. Look (John 4:35) – 'open your eyes and look at the fields!'

a. Biblically
We need to begin to see the world as Jesus sees it. We need to begin to see the peoples and nations of the world through his eyes and from his perspective. When Jesus saw the Samaritans coming towards him, dressed in their traditional white robes, he saw them with spiritual eyes (John 4:35). Elsewhere we are told that when Jesus saw the crowds, 'He had compassion on them, because they were harassed and helpless, like sheep without a shepherd' (Matt. 9:36). His disciples must have seen the same people with all their needs, but the difference between Jesus and his disciples was that he saw them from a

different spiritual perspective; and so must we.

First, we must regain our conviction that God's heart is for the nations – all the nations – of the world, and that it is God's command and will that we, his church, evangelise them. World mission, like local evangelism, is not an optional extra, it is a matter of the utmost importance.

Second, we must regain our conviction of the lostness of the lost and of the urgency of the hour. Men and women are not alright without the gospel. However cultured, sophisticated and educated they may be, without a personal experience of God through Jesus Christ, they are bound for hell – a conscious yet Christless eternity. It is not a popular, pleasant or palatable truth but it is a biblical one and we cannot shrink from it.

b. Geographically

We need to 'lift up our eyes', to get them off the narrow perspectives of our everyday lives and circumstances and look at the great harvest fields of the world. Every Christian should be interested in and fascinated by worldly news, not merely out of political or social concern, but out of a spiritual concern. How can we be concerned about the peoples of the world if we know nothing about them?

Remember, it was as William Carey accumulated his world facts and plotted them on his map that he saw, and increasingly felt, more and more clearly, the great need of the nations for the gospel.

We can use:

Current Events: As someone has said, 'The Bible tells us what God wants to do in the world; the newspaper tells us where he needs to do it and where we need to be involved through prayer.' We should be aware of what is going on in the world around us and turning that information into matters for prayer and concern for the world. Remember, what is going on in the world around us is all part of God's plan for the nations of the world. Scripture tells us that God has appointed Jesus *head over all things for the sake of the church* (Eph. 1:22), which means he is governing the affairs of the world in such a way that will ultimately be for the advancement of the gospel and the building up of the church.

Books: There are few things that stimulate an interest in mission better than accounts of what God has done in the past. Read the story of how the gospel has taken hold in a particular part of the world or among a specific tribe. Get hold of a good missionary biography, perhaps of one of the people previously mentioned in this book, and see how God has done extraordinary things through very ordinary people. One book that should be the indispensable companion of every Christian with any concern for the world is Patrick Johnstone's *Operation World*. This encyclopaedic analysis of the spiritual state and needs of every country of the world, organised in a helpful prayer diary format, is a must for the Christian with a world view.

Mission Literature: Why not subscribe to the magazine of one or two mission agencies? Get them regularly and read about what it is like to serve overseas, what are the opportunities and challenges.

Mission Conferences: Make a point of attending a conference where you will have the chance to hear firsthand from those working overseas about the work that God has called them into, and discover that missionaries are not super-spiritual saints, but men and women just like you and me who have responded to a call of God on their lives.

Missionaries: Get to know a missionary or missionary couple, perhaps from your town or city, who is currently working overseas, and write to them on a regular basis. Ask them about life as a missionary, working in a foreign culture, etc. etc.

One of the problems that faces Christians as they set out to get informed about world mission is, 'Where do I start?' The world is such a big place and the situations so diverse and difficult, where do I begin?

Here's a good maxim that used to be well known – '*Know something about everywhere and everything about somewhere.*' We should keep a wide awareness of the whole scene, but we can't be expected to know everything about everywhere. Prayerfully choose one area of the world – a continent, a country, a people group; or an area of the work – radio, Muslim, etc., and find out as much as you can about it. Keep a record of everything that you discover.

2. Pray (Matthew 9:38)

Serious looking and learning should always lead to prayer. The more we look at the world through God's eyes and see the great needs, the more we will be driven to our knees to pray for the work and for the workers. As Frank Houghton puts it in his great hymn, 'Facing a task unfinished that drives us to our knees.'

a. We need to pray because God is the Lord of the harvest.

'Prayer is our first work in the harvest. And the reason is not hard to find. It is this: the harvest has a "Lord". He oversees the harvest. Someone supplies the workers. Someone controls the progress. And that "someone" is God. Our first business is not to look at the size of the harvest. Our first business is to pray to our God.'[1]

b. We need to pray because this is spiritual warfare.

Our fight is not against flesh and blood but against the spiritual forces of darkness. God's work must be done by God's power, and God's power is released through prayer.

Here is an exciting account of how God actually used new converts in one missionary situation, to pray into the kingdom of God people in another country.

'David Howard was a missionary in Colombia, South America, when God seemed to be answering many, many prayers. New believers were everywhere! God worked mightily, and David rejoiced to see this fruit. But at the same time, David's older brother, Phil, toiled away amongst the Slavey Indians in Canada's northwest territories. Phil had worked with these Indians for fourteen years without one convert.

'One night, David shared his concern for his brother, Phil, with the Indians he was working with in Colombia. After sharing his concern, David sat down. The village leader rose and invited the people to pray. David describes what happened next: "He didn't have to repeat the invitation. Two hundred people went to their knees immediately and began to pray. Their custom is for all to pray out loud together .... That evening they prayed for one hour and fifteen minutes without stopping. They poured out their hearts for Phil and his wife, Margaret, and for those Canadian Indians."

'The Colombian Indians' concern for Phil continued long after their prayer session. They sent letters of encouragement and continued to pray.

'David Howard found out later that Phil, after fourteen years of ministry, had reached an all-time spiritual low. He was thinking, *What's the use?* He wondered why he should persevere. One night he went to bed defeated and discouraged, but the next morning he awoke with a new joy and courage to continue the work to which God had called him.

'When the two brothers compared dates, the times coincided exactly; the very night that Phil went to bed discouraged and awoke revived was the night that the Colombian Indians had spent time in zealous prayer on his behalf. And not only Phil's spirits were revived; in a short while, the Spirit began to work, and the first converts of the Slavey Indian tribe reported their decisions to Phil. By ones and twos they started to come, in answer to the prayers of others 4,000 or more miles away!'[2]

c. We need to pray for more workers.

The need is great. For many years, the number of those from the UK offering themselves for overseas service has been steadily declining, and yet the opportunities are great. To give just one example – AIM International could send out nearly 500 missionaries to Africa tomorrow to meet the requests of the national churches, but they are not there; there are too few willing to go.

d. We need to pray for the present workers.

How much does praying for missionaries figure in your prayer life? Not the casual, superficial 'God bless the missionaries' type of prayer, but real, fervent, engaging prayer, prompted and energised by the Spirit of God. One of the difficulties in praying for missionaries and other Christian workers who, perhaps, we don't see or hear from very often and can't identify with their situation, is keeping our prayers fresh and meaningful over a long period of time.

Let me make two suggestions which I have found to be helpful.

First, pray 'Biblical Prayers'. Some years ago I was challenged to use some of the prayers of, for example, the apostle Paul as a model for praying for myself and others. What a difference it made to my praying. Instead of praying very superficially and generally, often for material and circumstantial things, I found most of my praying taken up with timeless and spiritual needs. I may not know what my missionary friend is in particular need of today or what difficulties he may be facing, but I do know that he needs to be strengthened with power through God's Spirit in his inner being (Eph. 3:16); that the eyes of his heart need to be enlightened in order that he may know the hope to which he has been called (Eph. 1:18); that he needs the God of hope to fill him with all joy and peace (Rom. 15:13), and so on.

Secondly, the following guide to help in praying for missionaries has been suggested by my very good friend and colleague Timothy Alford, the previous UK Director of AIM International:

Sundays: S = Spirituality
Pray that the Lord's work will bear the hallmark of the Holy Spirit's direction and that his workers will be Spirit-filled.

Mondays: M= Ministry
Our primary work is preaching and teaching. Pray that the workers will not be deflected.

Tuesdays: T = Trials
Plead for the problem situations which cry out for the Lord's power and deliverance.

Wednesdays: W = Words
Pray for those who struggle with language study, communication and prayer letters.

Thursdays: T = Thanksgiving
Have a thanksgiving day every week. Let the Lord know that you take nothing for granted.

Fridays: F = Family
Missionary families are not exempt from today's tensions. Pray too for relationships within the missionary family and with all national colleagues.

Saturdays: S = Security
Pray for safety for those in danger from such things as sickness, travel, thieves, loneliness, stress, political unrest and spiritual warfare.

If you want to read more of the need and power of prayer in world mission, but from a missionary's perspective, then you could not do better than read *Mountain Rain*, the biography of James Fraser who worked among the Lisu people in China. See especially pages 169-170.[3]

e. Pray for the Unreached

One exciting way in which God is involving Christians and churches in mission work today, is in praying for the unreached peoples of the world. I have included a short section on this at the end of this book and would warmly commend it to you.

3. Go (Matthew 28:19-20)

The Great Commission of Christ to his church still stands. It has never been rescinded or altered.

The Lord of the harvest still wants men and women to respond to his call and to go; to leave home and country and reach others with the gospel. There is a definite call of God to be a missionary, but the call has already been given in general terms; we need to ask God not if he wants us to go, but *where*.

Every Christian should personally seek God and ask, 'Where do you want me to go?' Many have never asked God that question, perhaps because they are afraid of what the answer might be! Many have taken it for granted that they would settle down in their home country, have a career, raise a family, etc., etc. Oh, they are committed to their local church and local Christian work, but they have never asked God whether he might want to use them somewhere else, possibly more strategic.

Of course, we are not all called to go to the foreign mission field – but some are. Some are called to be missionaries in their place of secular employment and that is right and necessary. Others are called to be 'full-time' Christian workers in their homeland, and our own country is as godless and needy as many foreign nations. But some are called to spend their lives in the service of the gospel in another culture and in another part of the world and certainly, the opportunities and needs are far greater today overseas than at home.

Given the spiritually confused climate in which we live, it's worth stressing that there is such a thing as 'a call'. The general call of God to the apostles and through them to the church was given years ago, but it comes personally and specifically as we seek God's will for our lives. I would be so bold as to guarantee that if I were to ask any of the many missionaries I know personally who are working overseas, 'Why are you still there?', they would say that it is because at some point in the past, God told them to go there and he hasn't yet told them to go home. You see, the novelty factor of living and working in a different culture wears off very quickly; the stresses and strains of coping with a different climate and language soon take their toll; the spiritual attack quickens and were it not for the sense of God having called them to do a specific – and as yet unfinished task – most of them would be on the next plane home.

Sending agencies have a responsibility, along with the home church, to ensure as far as they are able under God, that those they accept for overseas service are indeed truly called of God for that work. The cost of neglecting this issue is enormous.

How do I recognise this call?

Well, first of course, we must ask God if he has one for us. Perhaps we have not because we ask not. One AIM missionary is on the field today because her pastor challenged his congregation with the words, 'Give God the chance to turn you down.' She did and God didn't! The key is availability. I suspect many Christians never give God the chance to turn them down because they are afraid that he won't.

The whole area of guidance and recognising the call of God is of such importance that it merits a series of studies on its own, but I would suggest that God will use the following factors in the life of a Christian who is concerned to do his will, and when they all seem to come together, then we ought to consider very seriously what God might be saying to us.

Concern for the plight of the lost. Jesus was 'moved with compassion' when he looked on the crowds. God will not use us if we are not concerned. Do you feel something of the imbalance between the many opportunities you have to hear the gospel and the plight of millions who have yet to hear it for the first time?

Caution. An emotional response is not sufficient and can, by itself, be dangerous. We need guidance and confirmation from the Scriptures as a check. We should look to God to speak to us as we pursue our normal, regular reading of God's Word and attend the ministry of the Word in our local fellowship.

Consecration. Guidance must rate very near the top of the list of issues Christians most commonly have difficulty with. God has promised to guide us, but, on our part, certain conditions have to be met in order to receive and understand that guidance. Read, for example, Psalm 25:9 and 12: '*He guides the humble in what is right and teaches them his way ... Who, then, is the man that fears the LORD? He will instruct him in the way chosen for him*' and see who it is that God promises to guide ... the one who is humble and fears God. See Romans 12:1-2: 'Therefore, I urge you, brothers, in view of God's mercy, to offer your bodies as living sacrifices, holy and pleasing to God – this is your spiritual act of worship. Do not conform any longer to the pattern of this world, but be transformed by the renewing of your mind. *Then you will be able to test and approve what God's will is – his good, pleasing and perfect will.*' It is as we live lives set apart for God, we will more easily be able to discern and recognise God's will for us. The biggest problem we have with guidance is that we don't live close enough to the Lord to recognise his voice when he speaks to us.

Confidence in God. It is God's responsibility to give us guidance and direction. God already has a plan for us and good works which he has prepared for us to do. 'Trust in the LORD with all your heart and lean not on your own understanding; in all your ways acknowledge him, and he will make your paths straight' (Prov. 3:5-6). 'For we are God's workmanship, created in Christ Jesus to do good works, which God prepared in advance for us to do' (Eph. 2:10). What a comfort it is to know that God has got everything worked out for us and will, in his time and his way, reveal it to us.

Character. Are we disciplined by nature, able to adjust to a different culture, able to cope, perhaps, with a very basic lifestyle, etc.? Are we mentally and physically fit; emotionally and spiritually mature?

Contribution. Sometimes God confirms his call by making us aware that a particular gift, experience or ability is needed somewhere. A need, in and of itself, never constitutes a call, but it is often a vital ingredient. If you think God may indeed be calling you into mission service, it is worth asking several agencies whether and where they could use your particular skills.

Circumstances must be considered. We need to take account of such things as health and family responsibilities. While these things must never become obstacles to obedience and are under the control of our sovereign God, yet it would be foolish and unwise to disregard them.

Consultation. We need to share with, and learn from, other believers; pray with them and ask their counsel. We need to consult with those who know about missions and missionary service; contact mission agencies and read their magazines; speak or write to serving and former missionaries; attend mission conferences.

Church. We should talk and pray with our pastor and other spiritual leaders. Our sense of call should be tested and confirmed by the local church. One of the God-given responsibilities of church leaders is to recognise and bring out the gifting and calling of God in those entrusted to their care. In fact the weight of New Testament evidence suggests that the initiative should come from the church rather more than from the individual as we are used to today. I have stopped counting the times when, having suggested to someone that they speak to their pastor about their growing sense of call, they have been met with the response of, 'I wondered when you'd come and talk about this'. I only wish more church leaders took the initiative and spoke first to their members who they sensed God was calling out for service.

Conviction. Guidance often comes as a gradually growing inner conviction, so that we cannot get away from what we sense God is saying to us.

There comes a point in this whole issue where we have to take some action. There is an old Chinese proverb which says something along these lines – 'the journey of a thousand miles begins with the first step.' God will not mislead you if he knows that your heart and will are set on finding and obeying his perfect will for your life. As you begin to 'knock' on and 'push' at different doors of enquiry, you can be sure that he will keep the wrong doors firmly shut and only open the ones which will lead you a little further down the path to where he wants you to be.

Notes
1. Tom Wells, *A Vision for Missions*, Banner of Truth, p. 138.
2. Quoted by Paul Borthwick in *A Mind for Missions*, Navpress, pp. 63-64.
3. Eileen Crossman, *Mountain Rain*, OMF Books.

PRAYING FOR THE UNREACHED

One of the exciting ways in which God has been working in recent years, has been in response to the prayers of his people for the unreached peoples of the world. Much of this has come about as a result of efforts like the Adopt-a-People Programme (which has been embraced by a number of mission agencies).

The purpose behind this programme is to get churches and groups of praying Christians to commit themselves to persevering and believing prayer for an 'adopted' unreached people, somewhere in the world. This involvement should not be taken lightly. Like parents who adopt children into their family, with responsibility for that child until he/she is old enough to be independent, this is a long-term commitment and desire to see the task accomplished – a growing church established, not dependent on outside help, and evangelising its own people.

Churches which have wanted to get involved in world mission and have not been sure where to start have found this approach a good way of being in at the very beginning of a work among an unreached people, and have had the enormous excitement and joy of seeing so many of their prayers answered. Other churches, up to their eyes in mission commitment, have found this a helpful way of further expanding their vision and involvement without additional financial responsibilities.

The work of the Adopt-a-People programme is very much that of prayer. Prayer that God would raise up cross-cultural missionaries – either from within the country of the unreached people or from elsewhere; prayer that God would prepare the hearts and minds of the people to whom the missionaries will go with the precious word of life; prayer for the pulling down of Satan's strongholds that have, for generations, held men and women captive; prayer that God would build his church among the people to the eternal glory of his own name.

If you would like more information about the Adopt-a-People Programme, may I suggest that you write, either to

The Adopt-a-People Co-ordinator
Africa Inland Mission International
2 Vorley Road
Archway
London N19 5HE
E-mail: adopt-a-people@aim-eur.org

or

Interlinks
PO Box 210
West Drayton
Middlesex
UB7 8NN
E-mail: joanrogers@xc.org

MY PERSONAL COMMITMENT

Responding to all that I have learned from God through His Word, I will, with His help

- regularly and intelligently pray for the needs and workers of His mission field

- seriously begin to learn 'something about everywhere and everything about somewhere'

- establish contact with a serving missionary or couple, begin to correspond with them, and be committed to praying for them

- subscribe to and read carefully a missionary magazine and turn the information to prayer

- read a missionary biography

- ask God what part He would have play in this great work

- regularly evaluate my progress, re-establish or set new goals, and renew this commitment

Signed:
Date:

RECOMMENDED READING

Indispensable Handbooks:
Operation World Patrick Johnstone (OM)
You can change the world Jill Johnstone (OM)
You too can change the world Daphne Spragget (OM)

Books about World Mission:
The Church is Bigger Than You Think Patrick Johnstone (CFP)
Territorial Spirits and World Evangelisation Chuck Lowe (Mentor/OMF)
Let the Nations Be Glad John Piper (IVP)
A Hitch-Hiker's Guide to Mission Ada Lum (IVP/STL)
A Mind for Missions Paul Borthwick (NavPress)
Don't just stand there . . . Martin Goldsmith (IVP)
Love your local missionary Ed. Martin Goldsmith STL/MARC/EMA
Mission Today Graham Cheesman Qua Iboe
Serving as Senders Neal Pirolo OM
The Challenge of Missions Oswald J. Smith Marshall Pickering
The Great Omission Robertson McQuilkin Baker
The World Christian Starter Kit Glen Myers WEC/STL
Tinker, Tailor, Missionary? Michael Griffiths IVP/OM
A Vision for Missions Tom Wells Banner of Truth
What on earth are you doing? Michael Griffiths IVP
The Great Commission T. Omri Jenkins Evangelical Press
Why Bother with Mission? Stephen Gaukroger IVP

Missionary Biographies:
A Man in Christ (Hudson Taylor) Roger Steer OMF
Beyond the Minarets (Henry Martyn) Kellsye Finnie STL

Faithful Witness (William Carey) Timothy George IVP

We Felt Like Grasshoppers (AIM) Dick Anderson Crossway Books

Five Pioneer Missionaries Banner of Truth

Mountain Rain (James O Fraser) Eileen Crossman OMF

No Sacrifice too Great (C T Studd) Eileen Vincent WEC/OM

Storming the Golden Kingdom (Judson) John Waters IVP/STL

Through Gates of Splendour (Jim Elliot) Elisabeth Elliott OM

Love Breaks Through (Katie MacKinnon) Katie MacKinnon CFP

Failure is not Final (Janny van der Klis) Janny van der Klis Marshall Pickering

A Hundred Houses (Irene Rowley) Anne Rayment CFP

A Fistful of Heroes John Pollock CFP

Faith on Fire (Norman Grubb) Stewart Dinnen CFP

Hudson and Maria (Hudson Taylor) John Pollock CFP

Jack of All Trades, Mastered by One (Jack Selfridge) Jack Selfridge CFP

A PRAYER

Give me a vision, Lord, I plead,
Vision of souls and a world in need:
Loved ones and friends – the one next door;
Then let me see there are millions more.

Give me a vision, Lord Divine,
Kindle with fire this cold heart of mine;
May with unselfishness it burn,
Fill me with love and a deep concern.

Give me a vision, Lord Divine,
So charged with power that it shall shine
Out to the lost in their deepest night,
Wand'ring alone in their sad, sad plight.

Give me a vision, Lord Divine,
Without a limit or boundary line;
Help me to see a world in sin,
Not just the field I am working in.

Give me a vision, heart-stirring vision,
Open my eyes, Lord, today:
Show me the sighing; the doomed and the dying;
Give me a vision I pray.

AIM

reaching Africa's peoples ...
serving Africa's churches

Africa Inland Mission International is a long-established mission agency, committed to reaching the peoples of Africa with the gospel of Jesus Christ, and to assisting African churches grow to maturity. An interdenominational, protestant mission agency with an evangelical basis of faith, its primary purpose is to plant churches in unevangelised areas, through direct evangelism, Scripture translation, literature distribution and other related ministries. Alongside these ministries goes its work of serving the church through leadership training and theological education.

Founded in 1895 by Peter Cameron Scott with the purpose of reaching Africa for Christ, it now has a membership of over 800 men and women, working in cooperation with a number of national churches of different denominations in fifteen countries of East and Central Africa, and the islands of the Indian Ocean.

Countries of service (in historical order of entry) are :

- Kenya
- Tanzania
- Democratic Republic of Congo (formerly Zaire)
- Uganda
- Central African Republic

- Sudan
- Comores
- Seychelles
- Madagascar
- Namibia
- Réunion
- Mozambique
- Lesotho
- Chad
- Angola

Ministries include:

- Church planting & Evangelism
- Theological Education & Leadership
  Development
- Scripture Translation, Literature & Literacy
- Medical/Health Care
- Development
- Education – National & Missionary Schools
- Radio/Media
- Aviation, Building and Engineering
- Urban & Youth Work
- Administration

AIM's members come from churches across the world. In recent years, the Mission has experienced a number of evacuations of personnel from various African countries where civil wars are in progress.

Despite many years of gospel witness, Africa still presents many challenges: there are many openings for flexible and mature Christians to work as evangelists and church planters in remote areas and for people with theological training to help with Theological Education. Contact Angela Godfrey, the Associate Personnel Director, at

2 Vorley Road
London
N19 5HE
tel: 0171 281 1184
email: enquiry@aim-eur.org

Born and brought up in a missionary family in India, John Brand lives with his wife Caroline and teenage sons in central Scotland. Having pastored churches in London and Liverpool, he is now UK Director of Africa Inland Mission International and exercises a preaching and teaching ministry throughout UK, Europe and parts of Africa.